Sunflower in the sky
and other poems

Matias Sayko

Kindle

ISBN-13: 9798834962397
ISBN-10: 1477123456

Cover design by: Matias Sayko
Library of Congress Control Number: 2018675309
Printed in the United States of America

To my son, Francisco.

Sunflower in the sky

Yelling my successes and my deserts

Yelling with echoes, threatening the sky.

Squeezing the throat to curse a cloud.

I don't want the echo to come back,

It loses the strength of my lungs.

I want to yell standing up

because my sunflower is setting on fire now,

my precious yellow flower cries in tiny bell sounds.

And I yell at the dawn,

Yell at the sunset,

Yell at the eagles,

Yell in my battle.

It feels silent

but I need to get rid of my anger,

get off this body,

yelling nothing,

until the words I forgot re-appear.

I unfold my voice

and I begin to be free.

SILENCE

Silence comes down through the mountain

As if it was water

Interrupted only by the singing of birds

It looks at itself in the mirror of a lake

And continuous its way.

The spirits go along with it

In its descent,

They have no shape

But they smell like heat.

Nobody sleeps with this virtuous sound.

The shadows shape it

And the lake gives it wings.

To the beat of the wind,

In the frozen water

And in a hug made of clouds

It dances.

And on the tip sleeps a child,

An Angel who traces,

With his dreams,

Sheets of music

That the birds read

While they sing.

SPARKLE

The air brings your memory,

The scent of the rain and

The smell of wet grass

Shelter me from your absence.

In each water drop I hear your voice

Like a rattle or an harp.

Your fingerprints are like stars

They go jogging through the Space at night.

And your eyes

Are the breath of Spring.

But since we are in Winter,

With an unexpected and fierce wind

You hug me,

Without a warning.

Son,

The distance is mute at times,

But the heart beats strong

Like the jump of a fire spark.

I see you driving your celestial body in the middle of the night,

Thank you, baby

You taught me how to

Love a star.

LENNY

So now my glasses are full of dirt,

I can see your fingerprints everywhere.

Rubbing them with my t-shirt will

Make it worse.

So I see you.

And

I don't miss you

… that's nonsense.

It's only that when momma called me out,

You were always a good support,

Or when daddy left home

You were always there for me, listening.

They laughed at me in school

Because you were there,

But they don't get it.

I hate that I'm not gonna take you

To the summer vacay though

But it's okay,

You live in my heart now.

Momma thought it would be a good idea

To send you as a gift to the kids in-need

And I grabbed you very tight but now

All I have is your dirt in my glasses

And I hate when that happens.

And I'm not a kid as they say,

It's just that, Lenny, you were

The best Teddy Bear,

my one and only friend.

THE HUMMINGBIRD

Asleep on the top of an almond tree

He made his bed:

He used a fruit as a pillow

And a leaf as a blanket,

To shelter from the dew.

One squirrel looked at him,

But didn't attack him.

Perplexed,

She decided to sing him a soothing song.

The hummingbird dreamt

He was part of a flock

To not be always on his own,

So he felt comforted.

But hey!

He doesn't know he can see more colors

Than us humans,

He can fly in all directions

And, most of all,

Dream while a squirrel

Sings him a lullaby.

THUNDER

I

Rescue my remains and

Put them on the kitchen counter.

Next, I prepare the main table with delight

Until it is exquisitely decorated.

I wear a vulture mask I ordered online

And command my remains.

They are ordered with care

Like an A+ math exam of 9th grade.

I turn on the light

And we look at each other (my remains and I)

Unexpectedly, in the stillness of silence

I colonize my unknown self.

And though I see myself as a foreigner,

I take off the mask, put it aside,

And with tears of joy

I embrace and celebrate what's left of me.

I write words you wouldn't understand

In the air.

Like little feet in the sea, thunder, tree.

They evaporate,

My mouth makes no sound,

My eyes, thirsty, listen

And my ears touch the

Flutter of my angel.

MISS CHI

I loved my shoes.

Miss Chi gave them to me.

I didn't like my old shoes with its ends opened

like an hippopotamus mouth

Showing my fingers out.

I loved my shoes.

But momma sold them.

I told Miss Chi about it

and she gave an angry look.

I loved my shoes

because they brought magic to my home.

Momma always makes these noises with the bottles, specially

at night,

when I pretend I'm sleeping.

Yes, I loved my shoes

but momma needed the money

to buy more bottles to make that sound

to call angels,

I'm sure she wants them close to us.

WINNING

It happened to me from the top of this wrinkled day,

through mists and fogs,

darkness and smoke,

that I won.

But I didn't.

I mean, indeed I win,

But I don't need that occasional light,

I refuse to be that person.

So I arrived home winning,

but still listening the cries in the distance,

the glimpses of an unknown nostalgia,

stars made of the opaque

drowning in words.

I lost my sky,

and with my just flooded soul

I couldn't find sense.

But its not me writing,

the paper does it,

the words come and go for a walk,

I'm a horrible poet

I wish this words could stop

but they are annoying and infatuated.

But I don't identify myself with me,

I am the debris,

I identify myself with syntactic analysis,

with an open sachet scattered on the market. Nobody wants it,

And I find it so romantic.

Now I'm all that's left from my name.

An M, a T and I forgot what else.

RAMONA

The afternoon is clean

like an empty leaf

like the summer-look

in a forgotten town in northern Argentina.

She writes poems on the ground

with a stick or with her feet.

She escapes, she unlocks,

designing words with stones.

Very remotely she gets a paper from a stranger, from the

unknown.

She cries in words

written in the ground

And blown away by the wind.

Then she runs and runs,

to forget,

runs before the hope gets cold.

And when she gets home,

she wishes it was a shelter.

Yet, she takes off her backpack

Which she handcrafted to get rid of despair

That's her most exquisite fabric

Because it means the night has arrived.

She lays down on her bed,

Listening to the sound of crickets and owls.

In her sleep she finds safety

Just like in her words made of stone

She dreams now and smiles.

WOLF IN THE NIGHT

The victim appears.

Jump.

Bite.

Bloody snow.

A frightened bullet from afar,

Sticks into his body

Until his eyes become blind.

His human executioner

Grabs him from the tail.

He lies on his back

Watching the Earth from above.

The whisper of his mother

Suddenly brings shelter

And he howls from the sky

So softly

Like an ángel.

4 AM

My shadow got curved

Since that summer you flew away

In brief signs of the soul you explained me you were here, but.

But————————

In a blue sigh I let you go.

It is nighttime and I lay a book in my legs,

They create a tent.

I'd like that tent to be in our bed

To assist your crying

Now dissolved in nature.

Through a light vertex, Destiny fell

And told me the bitter news.

Then my angel opens his mouth

To pour some warmth,

To let me know, one more time, he is here

Beyond the imprisoned margins of us human beings.

MALIBU

The wind coming from the sea

Brought that special smell of Bliss today.

You woke up early

Just like yesterday

To throw snails

You collect from the shore and throw into the sea, YAY!

And I'm watching you through the window

I wonder what's going on in your mind while you play

But dear Lord, thank you, I'm not a snail…

You brought the sea to my feet

The pleasure I find today

Keeps my demons away.

Nobody, except me, woke up early watching you slip snails,

Watching you play

I'm so chilled I think I will

Accelerate my steps

So that my memory doesn't catch me,

And I don't remember about yesterday.

WAVES

Silence.

Everyone hears it in their own way.

Silence

Is like water:

It can nurture

Or it can drown you.

I listen to the wind trying to find something.

The waves come and go.

And I would like to hear your voice,

To prove you are close.

At that point a wave wets my feet

To shorten some kind of distance.

That's when I know

Beyond knowing,

It is you who speaks

in waves

to me.

So, I jump into the sea

And start to swim.

I no longer need words,

It's just you,

The sea

And me.

AGAIN, AND AGAIN

And suddenly the grief runs over me

like a truck hits a rabbit.

The siren turns on,

reminds me it's still time to fight.

A decay anguish,

because I don't want to use it, I'd rather let it go.

It's not that I haven't travelled it before,

It's only that I

Don't

Want

To

Feel it

Again.

You've disinterestedly learned how to fly

Even before saying pa

And I'm all clumsy, short of breath

when I go for a little walk.

I look at you:

when I look inside.

I hear you:

when I listen beyond the sound.

I caress you:

when the wind presses me out.

And it's not that the sorrow has gone, no, no,

It lives here,

But you live past the high, eternal

like the sky.

Much wiser than the sun,

fresher than the flapping of a hummingbird flight.

I want to be like you, one day

Not only to hug you, or to be together,

but to tell you, more frequently

I

LOVE

YOU

     I

     LOVE

     YOU

          I

          LOVE

          YOU

My little sunflower in the sky.

NO MATTER

HOW DELICATE

The mornings are

THEY ARE

CORROSIVE

For us

WHO ARE

On pause.

ACKNOWLEDGEMENT

Thank you everybody.
But most of all,
thank you Mom and Dad.

UNTITLED

(Here you can write your own poem
or the list of the grocery store)